CATCH THE BUTCHER

Adam Seidel

BROADWAY PLAY PUBLISHING INC
New York
www.broadwayplaypublishing.com
info@broadwayplaypublishing.com

CATCH THE BUTCHER
© Copyright 2018 Adam Seidel

First edition: February 2018
I S B N: 978-0-88145-755-1

Book design: Marie Donovan
Page make-up: Adobe InDesign
Typeface: Palatino

CATCH THE BUTCHER was first produced by Panndora Productions in 2013 at the Long Beach Playhouse. The cast and director were:

NANCY.. Karen Wray
BILL .... Derrick Long
JOANNE..Rebecca Taylor

Director .... Chrisanne Blankenship-Billings

CATCH THE BUTCHER received its Off-Broadway premiere at Cherry Lane Theatre in 2015. The cast and director were:

NANCY... Lauren "Luna" Velez
BILL .... Jonathan Walker
JOANNE...Angelina Fiordellisi

Director .... Valentina Fratti

CHARACTERS & SETTING

BILL, *early to mid 40s*
NANCY, *early to mid 40s*
JOANNE, *mid to late 50s*

Anywhere, Texas. Present day.

Places:

A park
A basement
The upstairs common area of a house

NOTE ON LOCATIONS AND SCENIC CHANGES

There are two significant scenic changes in the play. Scene 3 to 4 from park to basement and Scene 8 to 9 from basement to upstairs. In my opinion theses changes are best achieved with a minimal approach. Here is a suggestion for each setting.

Park— A bench.

Basement— A chair. A tray on wheels for tools.

Upstairs— A couch. A round dining room area with a table and four chairs.

The one thing that should always be constant throughout the show is a door, which is preferably built into the upstage wall, and you can interpret "door" however you like. In the basement it can be used as the portal to upstairs. Upstairs, it can be used as the entrance to the basement. All other entrances "upstairs" can be imagined stage right or left.

A NOTE ON STABBINGS

I'd like the stabbings to seem as real as possible. You want the audience to actually scream or gasp. You want the play to be funny, because it is, but you also want the element of horror to be present as well.

I'd like to give a shout to a few folks whose help, love, support and guidance have gotten me where I am. Panndora Productions, thank you. Valentina Fratti, thank you. Angelina Fiordelisi, thank you. Mom, thank you. And above all, to Chelsea my wife, thank you.

Scene 1

(It is morning on a sunny day. We are in a typical park.)

(NANCY, a plainly dressed woman in her mid forties, is sitting on a bench quietly reading a book. She turns the page.)

(After a few moments BILL, a decent looking guy in his mid forties enters. He stands at a distance from NANCY, watching her.)

(After a moment, NANCY looks up from her book and looks at BILL. She smiles at him. BILL looks away. NANCY returns to her book. She turns the page.)

(A moment passes and BILL once again looks at NANCY. He even takes a small step in her direction. NANCY seems aware of this yet doesn't react. BILL senses NANCY's awareness and backs away. Then after a moment he exits. NANCY looks to where he exits. She goes back to her book. She turns the page.)

(Lights fade.)

Scene 2

(The next day but it is later. Perhaps nearing the end of sunlight. NANCY is sitting at the same bench. She is now reading a magazine listening to a small portable speaker, which is lightly playing twangy country music.)

(After a moment, BILL enters, now dressed in a camouflage coat. They look at one another for a moment. BILL, looking like he got his hand stuck in the cookie jar, slowly exits.)

(NANCY sighs and returns to her magazine.)

(Lights fade.)

Scene 3

(The next day, but now it is night time. NANCY is sitting at the same bench. She is now listening to earbuds and reading.)

(BILL, now wearing a ski mask, slowly enters from behind NANCY. He walks up behind her and she pretends not to notice.)

(BILL grabs NANCY, covering her mouth. NANCY resists, but BILL has complete control. BILL puts a towel over NANCY's face and after a few moments she succumbs and passes out.)

(Lights fade.)

Scene 4

(It is the next morning. We are inside BILL's house, in his basement. NANCY is sitting tied up in a chair, her mouth gagged. In the rear is a tray table similar to the kind seen in a surgical suite , and on the back wall is a shelf containing heavy duty tools. After a moment we hear a thick metal door open and he enters. He rolls the cart over to her. Then he goes to a shelf on the back wall, and selects tools. He brings them to the tray, then goes to her and takes off her gag.)

BILL: I want you to do something for me.

NANCY: What?

BILL: Scream.

NANCY: You want me to scream?

BILL: As loud as you can.

NANCY: Ahhh.

BILL: Louder.

NANCY: AHH.

BILL: LOUDER.

NANCY: AAAAAAHHHHHHHHHHHHHHHHHhhh…

BILL: Has anyone told you, you have a wonderful scream?

NANCY: No.

BILL: Well, you do. It's savage. Primal.

NANCY: Thank you?

BILL: Do you know why I told you to scream?

NANCY: I can take a guess.

BILL: I'd be delighted if you did.

NANCY: You want to make a point that no one will hear me.

BILL: And why would I want that?

NANCY: Because you want me to give up hope.

(Pause)

BILL: Do you know who I am?

NANCY: I have some idea.

BILL: Who am I?

NANCY: You're the butcher of Harbour Park.

BILL: Got it on the first try.

NANCY: Though I don't know why they call you that.

BILL: I think it's pretty straightforward. I started my illustrious career in Harbour Park, which is where I got you. But you're right. Now I kill women all over the city.

NANCY: Eleven in total. The past few up in Galaxy square.

BILL: You follow my work.

NANCY: How did I get here?

BILL: I brought you.

NANCY: But how? The last thing I remember I was sitting in the park.

BILL: I put a rag soaked in chloroform over your mouth. That made you pass out. Then I dragged you to my car, drove here, and voila.

NANCY: I thought it would be more intricate.

BILL: Sorry to disappoint you.

NANCY: Would you mind if I asked you a personal question?

BILL: That depends on how personal.

NANCY: Why do you kill women?

BILL: It doesn't matter.

NANCY: I think it matters a lot.

BILL: I don't care what you think.

NANCY: Do you hate women?

BILL: Women are an essential component to society. Without them man would be screwed.

NANCY: If you feel that way then why do you kill us?

BILL: Because I enjoy it.

(*Pause.* NANCY *takes in the tray of tools next to her.*)

NANCY: So what's all that?

BILL: My tools. For your sake and mine, I want to do this correctly. In order to do that, I need to have the proper tools.

For example, when pulverizing an extremity, such as am arm or a leg, I'll need a proper hammer.

Or if I'm going to be cutting something like say, a tendon or a jugular vein, I'll need a very sharp knife. And of course, no party is complete without a trusty screwdriver.

(NANCY *takes in the more heavy duty implements on the rear shelf.*)

NANCY: Those other tools. What are they for?

BILL: These? (*Holding up the chisel and saw*) These are for if I start to feel creative. You know the old saying. "You never know when you'll need a rusty handsaw."

NANCY: I've never heard that saying.

BILL: That's because I just made it up. (*He resumes arranging the tools on the tray in a very specific way.*)

NANCY: You're very particular about your tools.

BILL: Guilty as charged.

NANCY: Is that part of your ritual?

BILL: I've always been obsessed with organization. I can thank my mother for that.

NANCY: Do you and your mother have a good relationship?

BILL: We used to.

NANCY: But not any more?

BILL: No.

NANCY: May I ask why?

BILL: Because she's dead.

NANCY: ...Oh.

BILL: I didn't kill her if that's what you're thinking.

NANCY: I wasn't.

BILL: She died of a heart attack. The woman loved cheese. Excessively. I told her to watch out. That a person can only eat so much cheese before it has adverse effects, but did she listen? Of course not. And now she's dead.

NANCY: I guess she should have listened.

BILL: Yes. She should have. Is that what you were thinking?

NANCY: What?

BILL: That I killed my mother?

NANCY: No.

BILL: It's alright if you did. I could see how you would given who I am and—

NANCY: I didn't.

(A very slight moment is shared, which is broken by BILL *disengaging.)*

NANCY: If you don't mind, may I ask you something else?

BILL: Shoot.

NANCY: Why did you abduct me?

BILL: Because you were there.

NANCY: But you didn't take me right away.

BILL: I needed to study you first.

NANCY: Study me how?

BILL: I had to decide whether or not you were worthy.

NANCY: Of being murdered?

BILL: Of my attention.

NANCY: Am I?

BILL: You wouldn't be here if you weren't.

NANCY: What criteria is my worthiness based on?

BILL: You are naive. And that makes you easy prey. According to the rules of natural selection, people like you get picked off the herd first.

NANCY: So I'm here because I'm weak.

BILL: You're also very beautiful. But I'll bet you already knew that. People who are always do. It's the way you all walk around. The way you carry yourselves. Like you can feel us looking at you. Admiring you're beauty.

NANCY: You're the first person to tell me that.

BILL: That you're naive?

NANCY: That I'm beautiful.

(Pause. BILL resumes arranging his tools.)

NANCY: Do you ever feel alone?

BILL: What?

NANCY: Doing what you do, I imagine life gets lonely.

BILL: Being alone suits me.

NANCY: Why?

BILL: I don't like people.

NANCY: Because people say you're a delusional psychopath?

BILL: Because people are assholes.

NANCY: People are assholes when they fear things.

BILL: What about you? Are you afraid?

(Pause)

NANCY: Do you ever think about death?

BILL: All the time.

NANCY: I meant do you think about yours.

BILL: Never.

NANCY: I think about mine. Every morning I wake up and I feel like I'm missing something. I lay there staring at the ceiling and I have this feeling that the time I've spent on the Earth has meant absolutely nothing and I will be completely forgotten. I wonder if I'll feel like that when I'm dead.

BILL: *(Softly)* I don't know.

(Pause)

NANCY: I asked why you kill women and you responded that it gives you pleasure.

BILL: I said I enjoyed it.

NANCY: Enjoyment and pleasure are the same thing.

BILL: What's your point?

NANCY: Don't take this the wrong way, but that comment struck me as a little bit mindless.

BILL: I hope you're not calling me mindless.

NANCY: Just the opposite. You seem very mindful and that's why that comment surprised me. The pursuit of pleasure is driven by impulse, not thought. You seem deeper than that. More complex. *(Beat)* Can I tell you a secret?

BILL: Sure.

NANCY: I've thought about being one of your victims. I've played how

you'd take me over and over in my head. *(Beat)* Would you like to hear about it?

(Beat)

BILL: Yes.

NANCY: It's near sunset. I'm walking through the park alone. Looking for a shortcut I stray from the main path. Soon I'm walking through the trees completely lost. Then I get this feeling like I'm being watched. So I start to walk faster, but the feeling gets stronger. I run faster but the faster I ran the stronger the feeling becomes until… it's just warmth. *(Beat)* That's when I wake up.

BILL: Was the real thing as good?

NANCY: It was better.

(A somewhat odd pause filled with tension. After a moment BILL *begins to laugh.)*

BILL: You are something else.

NANCY: In what way?

BILL: In the way you're trying to play me.

NANCY: I assure you I'm not—

BILL: It's not a problem. I actually find it quite entertaining.

NANCY: Why would I be playing you?

BILL: So you can escape. But I can assure you, that's not going to happen.

NANCY: I never said I'm trying to escape.

BILL: Very good. *(He begins to exit.)*

NANCY: Where are you going?

BILL: I need to go to work.

NANCY: When are you going to kill me?

BILL: When I return home this evening. Until then sit tight.

NANCY: My name is Nancy, by the way. In case you were wondering.

*(*BILL *returns to* NANCY *and puts the gag back on.)*

BILL: I wasn't.

(BILL *exits the room and closes the door.* NANCY *sits still. Lights fade.)*

Scene 5

(It is that night. NANCY *is sitting with the gag on. She is asleep. After a moment the metal door opens and* BILL *enters, now wearing an apron and rubber gloves. She watches him for a moment and then tries to speak through the gag.)*

NANCY: *(Muffled)* Ghfe fhsew fhhhfhfh

BILL: I'm sorry. I can't hear what you are saying.

NANCY: *(Muffled)* Hdhdhd dhdhhd ssssss

BILL: If you're going to speak with the gag on, you've got to pro-nun-ciate. *(He goes to* NANCY *and takes off the gag.)* Now, what is it?

NANCY: I need to use the powder room. *(Pause)*
NANCY: I said I—

BILL: I heard you the first time.

NANCY: So—

BILL: If you have to go you have to go.

NANCY: Here? In front of you?

BILL: I can turn around.

NANCY: I'd rather hold it.

BILL: Suit yourself. *(He goes to the tray of implements. He chooses a small knife.)* What do you know about the human body?

NANCY: I know that in order for it to function properly it needs to go to the bathroom.

BILL: Other than that.

NANCY: I know the basics, I guess.

BILL: Then let me ask you a question. How long would it take for me to drain all the blood from your body with this knife?

NANCY: You couldn't.

BILL: Why not?

NANCY: The more blood that leaves the system the more a person's blood pressure drops until the heart stops. When that happens there's usually still a pint to a pint and a half of blood left.

BILL: You know more than you let on.

NANCY: Back in college I had a roommate studying to be a nurse.

BILL: In that case, let me rephrase the question. If I were to cut you with this knife, how long would it take for you to bleed to death?

NANCY: It depends on where you cut me.

BILL: You got it. For example, if I cut your iliac, *(Holds knife to* NANCY's *inner thigh)* it might take four minutes. If I cut your brachial *(Holds the knife to* NANCY's *inside elbow)* It might take three to three and a half. But if I cut you here *(Holds the knife to her neck)* it would be much quicker yet far more painful.

NANCY: Is it true you rape your victims?

BILL: I beg your pardon?

NANCY: According to sources it's what you do.

BILL: …What sources?

NANCY: The Herald.

BILL: Is this about the article they printed last week? About how before I chop up my victims and throw them in the river I ritualistically rape them? *(Beat)* Is that what you want?

NANCY: I just want to know if it's true.

(Beat)

BILL: That story is nothing but filth and lies.

NANCY: I knew it. I just wanted to hear it from your mouth.

BILL: Thank you for the vote of confidence. Now I'm going to kill you.

(BILL puts the knife to NANCY's throat.)

NANCY: Before you do can I ask a favor? It's about your poems.

BILL: What about them?

NANCY: The Herald said you write one for each of your victims. Is that part filth and lies too?

BILL: That part's true. Why?

NANCY: The Herald published your last few poems.

BILL: I'm aware.

NANCY: Your words spoke to me. I thought before you chopped me up it might be nice to hear mine.

BILL: I haven't finished it.

NANCY: Would you mind sharing what you have?

BILL: Yes.

NANCY: Is that a yes as in you're going to share it or a yes as in you mind reading it? Cause I promise I won't laugh or anything. Even if it's bad. Not that it'll be bad—

BILL: Stop it.

NANCY: Stop what?

BILL: STOP SCREWING WITH ME.

NANCY: How am I screwing with you?

BILL: I'm holding a knife to your throat and you're asking me about my poems.

NANCY: So?

BILL: *So* you're supposed to be afraid of me!!!

NANCY: I can try to act more afraid if you like.

BILL: That's not what I—

NANCY: Help!

BILL: Shut up.

NANCY: If anyone can hear me I'm down here!

BILL: I said shut up.

NANCY: Help me!! Please! Somebody help meeee!!!!!

BILL: SHUT UP! SHUT UP! SHUUUT UUUP!

(Pause)

NANCY: If you're not going to kill me can I use the bathroom?

(BILL *puts the gag on* NANCY.)

BILL: Shut up.

(BILL *exits. Lights fade.*)

Scene 6

(It is an hour later. The room is now empty except for the chair, which has a handcuff dangling from the armrest. Door opens and BILL *enters, dressed the same way as before. He stares at the empty chair and is extremely tense. We hear the distant flush of a toilet.* NANCY *enters. Pause)*

NANCY: I know what you're going to say, and I can explain. I just really needed to go and it turns out you have a bathroom right there and—

BILL: How did you get free?

NANCY: Handcuffs are pretty easy to pick. All you have to do is flip the latch and I had a hair pin in my pocket and—

BILL: Sit down.

(NANCY *goes and sits in the chair.*)

NANCY: I've already told you I'm not going to run. If I was I would've—

BILL: Hold still.

NANCY: Did you want me to put the handcuffs back on?

(BILL *goes to shelf and pulls out a massive roll of duct tape.*)

BILL: Hold. Still.

(BILL *duct tapes* NANCY's *arms to the chair. When he's finished he puts away the tape.*)

BILL: Now I'm going to ask you some questions and I want yes or no responses. Understand?

NANCY: Yes.

BILL: Are you with the police?

NANCY: No.

BILL: Are you with the F B I?

NANCY: If I'm not with the Police then why would I be— No.

BILL: Are you a reporter?

NANCY: No.

BILL: Then who are you?

NANCY: My name is Nancy Rodgers. I'm originally from Wisconsin. I moved here to Texas with a guy I'd been dating a little over three years ago. He left. Now I live alone. I used to have a cat but he ran away.

BILL: Why are you here?

NANCY: Because you abducted me.

(BILL *picks up a handsaw from the tray and holds it to* NANCY'S *leg.*)

BILL: I'm going to ask you once more and if you don't tell me I'm going to cut your leg off. Now why are you here?

NANCY: I'll tell you. But first you have to do something for me.

BILL readies the saw.

NANCY: I'm not asking for much. I just want to know your name.

BILL: Why?

NANCY: So I know what to call you.

(BILL *pauses.*)

BILL: William.

NANCY: William. I like that name.

BILL: Great. Now tell me why you're here.

NANCY: Because I wanted to meet you.

BILL: Why?

NANCY: Everyone in the world sees what you do and they assume you're some monster or something. But I look at you and I see something else. I see a person who's just misunderstood.

BILL: I kill women, chop them up and throw them in the river!

NANCY: That is most certainly true. But you also write the most beautiful poetry I've ever read. It's tragic and sweet and everything poetry should be. Someone who writes poetry like that can't be all bad.

BILL: You are really starting to piss me off.

NANCY: I'm being serious. I think you and I have a lot in common and—

BILL: *You're insulting my intelligence.* And if you don't start giving me some straight answers—

NANCY: You want straight answers then here you go! I'm at the end of my rope. I had to meet you to see if you really were what they say you are. And if it ended up being true then you'd kill me which was fine because I had nothing left to lose.

BILL: I shouldn't have taken you.

NANCY: What?

BILL: I saw you in the park. The way you were sitting there, I knew you were waiting for me and I should have walked away.

NANCY: We can help each other. We can figure out what's gone wrong in our lives. What's turned us into these people. And we can fix it.

BILL: There is nothing to fix. This is the way I was born.

NANCY: Please. No one is born hating women.

BILL: Shut up!!

NANCY: Was it a bad breakup? Raised by controlling parents? Perhaps you're just a product of Catholic Education.

BILL: All the women I've killed are ugly. Their ugliness is a blemish on the world. I'm ridding the world of ugliness to make it a better place!

NANCY: You said I was beautiful.

(*Pause*)

BILL: Maybe I was lying.

NANCY: Or maybe you said it because you realize I understand you.

BILL: You're messing with me again and I told you not to.

NANCY: You don't have to be afraid of me, William.

BILL: Stop it.

NANCY: I'm not going to hurt you.

BILL: I'm warning you.

NANCY: I like you William. And I think you like me too!

(BILL *picks up a knife and jams it in* NANCY*'s leg.* NANCY *stares down at the knife in silent shock.*)

BILL: This is a very bad wound! And if you die from it, it's not my fault. *(He angrily exits and slams the door shut.)*

NANCY: *(Agony)* I'm sorry! *I'm sorrrrry…I'm* sorry….

(Lights fade.)

Scene 7

(It is two hours after the stabbing incident. NANCY *has passed out from the pain caused by the knife, still in her leg.* BILL *enters, not wearing the leather apron. He is carrying gauze and some other supplies. He goes to her, surveys the puncture wound. He pulls the knife out of her leg, and quickly compresses the wound. She lets out a slight moan. After a moment he tears her pants, and sees a huge scar running down her thigh. He pauses to study it. Lights fade.)*

Scene 8

(It is the next day. NANCY *is asleep. The wound is now covered and dressed well. Almost professionally.* BILL *enters with a tray of french toast that is garnished with flowers. He places it on the shelf and goes to inspect her wound. After*

doing so he begins to change the dressing. She wakes and looks at him. After a moment)

NANCY: How long have I been asleep?

BILL: Ten hours, two minutes and fifteen seconds. *(Pause)* How does your leg feel?

NANCY: It's really sore.

BILL: When I stabbed you I hit bone.

NANCY: Is that bad?

BILL: It can cause long term damage. *(Beat)* You'll be fine. I sutured the wound, gave you pain medication and antibiotics earlier this morning. Just needs a week or two and you'll be as good as new.

NANCY: Assuming you don't kill me first.

(BILL *looks at* NANCY *for a moment. Then he resumes changing the dressing. He finishes.)*

BILL: There.

NANCY: Wow. Very impressive.

BILL: It's nothing.

NANCY: Hardly. It's professional.

BILL: No it's not.

NANCY: If I didn't know any better I'd say you were a doctor.

(A pause)

BILL: I brought you food.

NANCY: What is it?

BILL: Texas French toast.

NANCY: You make it from scratch?

BILL: I didn't bake the bread, but yes. You hungry?

NANCY: Yes.

(BILL *begins to cut up the french toast so he can feed it to*
NANCY.)

BILL: Care for butter?

NANCY: Yes please.

BILL: Syrup?

NANCY: Only if it's the real stuff.

BILL: It is.

NANCY: Then yes.

(BILL *continues in silence. After a moment*)

BILL: When I was dressing your wound I noticed
something on your leg.

NANCY: Yes?

BILL: A scar.

NANCY: I guess it's hard to miss.

BILL: Where did it come from? *(Beat)* You don't have/
to tell me.

NANCY: It's fine./ I got it in a car accident.

BILL: It must have been very bad.

NANCY: It was.

BILL: Did it hurt?

NANCY: Yes. But it's alright. Pain doesn't bother me
anymore.

(*A silent moment is shared between them.* BILL *finishes
cutting the toast and brings plate to* NANCY.)

BILL: Here.

(BILL *begins to feed* NANCY *the french toast.*)

NANCY: Mmmm.

BILL: Good?

NANCY: Delicious. You're a very good cook.

BILL: You don't have to say that.

NANCY: I know I don't. But I mean it.

BILL: Water?

NANCY: Please.

(BILL *holds glass of water to* NANCY'S *lips and helps her drink. When she's done he sets the glass down on shelf.*)

NANCY: Would it be alright to call you something other than William?

BILL: What did you have in mind?

NANCY: I was thinking of Bill.

(*Pause*)

BILL: Listen. About before.

NANCY: You don't need to/ explain

BILL: You asked / if I wrote you a poem.

NANCY: Oh. Yes.

BILL: I finished it last night. And if you wouldn't mind I'd like to read it to you.

NANCY: Yes. Of course.

(BILL *reaches in his pocket and takes out a piece of paper.*)

BILL: When I'm done I'd like you to give me your honest opinion. Okay?

NANCY: Okay.

BILL: (*Beat*) It's titled "A single rose"…

A single Rose.

I look before me
and I where I once saw weeds
I now see
a single rose.

A single rose
that grew

from the dirt below.
A single rose
that in the sweetest voice
said hello.
A single rose
who when I cut it
from the ground
sprung feet
and began walking in my garden
to and fro.
A single rose
did grow and grow.
So I opened my gate
And I watched it go.

(Beat) What do you think?

NANCY: Honestly?

BILL: Yes.

NANCY: It's not your best work.

BILL: You don't like it?

NANCY: No. I do. But—

BILL: What?

NANCY: Well, it's not that it isn't good—I mean it's
not the worst thing I've ever heard. But it didn't really
rhyme—

BILL: Okay.

NANCY: And the repetition was a little on the
predictable side.

BILL: Alright—

NANCY: But not in a bad way.

BILL: I GET IT. *(Beat)* It's terrible.

NANCY: I didn't say it was terrible. /I just meant.

BILL: I know./ But it's boring. And meaningless.

NANCY: I don't think it's meaningless.

BILL: No?

NANCY: I just think you're feeling new emotions and you don't know how to express them.

BILL: What emotions?

NANCY: Well, I'm not you so I can't say. But to this point the poems you've written are about hate and pain. But now you're trying to write about- something else.

BILL: I've made a decision.

(BILL *gets a pair of scissors. He then goes to* NANCY.)

NANCY: About?

(BILL *lowers the scissors to* NANCY's *wrists and cuts the tape so her hands can go free.*)

BILL: I'm inviting you to come upstairs.

(BILL *turns around and exits, leaving the door open.* NANCY *sits rubbing her wrists.*)

Scene 9

(*It is minutes later. We are now in the upstairs of* BILL's *house, consisting of a living room area and a dining area. The breakfast tray is on the dining room table. He is sitting in the living room area, looking at the basement door, waiting. We hear footsteps slowly coming up a wooden staircase from the basement. After a moment, the basement door opens and* NANCY *enters.*)

BILL: Hi.

NANCY: Hi.

BILL: Would you care to get freshened up?

NANCY: That would be nice.

BILL: There's a bathroom down the hall. Plenty of fresh towels if you feel like showering.

NANCY: Thank you.

(*Pause*)

BILL: Feel free to use it whenever.

NANCY: I will. I just wanted to talk to you first.

(*Pause*)

BILL: Would you care to sit down?

NANCY: I'll stand if you don't mind.

BILL: That's fine.

NANCY: It's dark out.

BILL: It's just after eight.

NANCY: But you made me French Toast.

BILL: I've always been a fan of breakfast.

NANCY: So this is your house?

BILL: Yes.

NANCY: I like it.

BILL: I'm happy to hear it.

NANCY: Though it needs a little work.

BILL: What do you mean?

NANCY: I just mean it's a little behind the times.

BILL: It's vintage.

NANCY: I'll say. Especially the cabinets.

BILL: I'd prefer you not criticizing my cabinets.

NANCY: I'm not. Just they could use a woman's touch is all.

(*Pause*)

BILL: You said you wanted to talk.

NANCY: I did.

BILL: Then talk.

NANCY: I guess I can't help but wonder why you freed me.

BILL: Why do you think?

NANCY: Could be for a number of reasons.

BILL: Name some.

NANCY: Could be part of your game.

BILL: What game?

NANCY: The game you play with your victims. Make them feel like they're out of danger by freeing them and then when they come up stairs you—

BILL: I don't like to play games.

NANCY: Then perhaps you're just lying to me.

BILL: I'm many things, Nancy. But a liar I'm not.

NANCY: So you're not going to kill me?

BILL: No.

(Pause)

NANCY: You called me by my name.

BILL: Yes.

NANCY: I like the way you say it.

BILL: How do I say it?

NANCY: It makes me feel like someone knows I exist.

(NANCY puts her hand on BILL's shoulder. He stands and walks to different part of kitchen.)

NANCY: I'm sorry. I didn't mean to—

BILL: We done talking?

NANCY: I suppose we are.

BILL: Okay.

NANCY: So what comes next?

BILL: What comes next is you can take a shower if you wish.

NANCY: And then?

BILL: And then you are free to go.

NANCY: What do you mean?

BILL: I mean if I'm not going to kill you there's no point in you being here.

NANCY: But letting me go is taking an awfully big risk. What's to say I don't go straight to the police station?

BILL: I don't think you're going to do that.

NANCY: Look. I don't know you all that well but what if I stayed here?

BILL: You mean live here?

NANCY: I'm not messy. I'm good company.

BILL: Absolutely out of the question.

NANCY: I can be a great companion. I'm a real good listener.

BILL: Then listen to me now. I want you to leave.

NANCY: But I don't want to.

BILL: You just spent that past two days tied up in my basement!

NANCY: And what if I told you being tied up in your basement was the most exhilarating experience I've ever had?

BILL: *(Pointing towards area of the front door)* The front door is through there.

NANCY: Please, Bill.

BILL: Two blocks down there's a bus stop. That will take you downtown.

NANCY: Can we at least talk about it?

BILL fishes in his pocket and pulls out some change.

BILL: Here's fifty cents for the ride.

NANCY: Don't Hide your feelings.

BILL: I don't have feelings!!

NANCY: Of course you do. Look, I know why you've been doing what you do, Bill, and it sure isn't to rid the world of ugliness. You do it because you're punishing yourself.

BILL: How could you even begin to understand who I am or what I've done—

NANCY: I understand it because I do the same thing. Except I punish myself directly.

BILL: What are you talking about?

NANCY: I'm talking about the scar on my leg.

BILL: You said you got that in a car accident.

NANCY: I did. But it wasn't any accident. Two years ago I was driving down the road and I heard this voice in my head. It asked "Are you happy with who you are?" I'd always assumed I was. But that voice got me thinking. And I started looking at my life, who I was, where I was headed, and the more I thought about it the more I got scared. Because once I started peeling the layers back and I really looked at my life, I realized I had nothing, Bill. I was nothing. My existence consisted of buying things eating food being average. I was just another person sleep walking to their grave. So I decided to steer into a wall. And that's when it started.

BILL: When what started?

NANCY: My search for feeling something. Feeling anything. Even death if it came to that. It became an addiction that's consumed me ever since. And I've tried everything. Eating pills, drinking drain cleaner, walking into oncoming traffic. *(Beat)* I kept surviving and I couldn't understand why. But then I read your poems. And I knew the answer was with the man who wrote those beautiful words. Because he knew my emptiness. So I did everything I could to find you. Sat in every park, waited at every bus stop, walked down every abandoned trail. And then you came to me, Bill. Ever since you did that missing feeling is gone.

BILL: I'm giving you five seconds to walk out that door. And after that I'm taking you down to that basement and I'm chopping you up.

NANCY: I know it's only been a few days, but I love you Bill.

BILL: One.

NANCY: I do. With every fiber of my being. I feel like there's a force that's brought us together.

BILL: Two.

NANCY: I know you feel the same, Bill. I could see it in your eyes when you were tending to my wounds in that basement. No one has ever looked at me like that. We are soul mates.

BILL: Three.

NANCY: Dammit Bill! Stop and listen to me. I'm talking about us.

BILL: Four.

NANCY: Fine. You don't want to listen then kill me. But you and I know we were made for one another and nothing is going to change that.

BILL: FIVE.

(BILL *grabs a knife from breakfast tray and goes to* NANCY. *He stands poised to hack her to pieces. After a moment he drops the knife.*)

BILL: I can't do this.

NANCY: Look at me.

BILL: I can't.

NANCY: LOOK AT ME DAMMIT.

(BILL *looks at* NANCY.)

NANCY: This is our chance to set things right. But you need to let me in. I want to be with you.

BILL: I want to be with you too.

NANCY: Do you love me, Bill?

(*Beat*)

BILL: Yes.

NANCY: You do?

BILL: Since I first laid eyes on you I knew there was something about you. Like I found my other half.

NANCY: Oh Bill!

(NANCY *and* BILL *kiss.*)

BILL: This is crazy!

NANCY: We're proving the world wrong. We're showing everybody that we can take something negative and turn it to something positive. We can transform our ugliness into beauty. But before we can we have to make a promise to one another.

BILL: What?

NANCY: What is in the past is in the past and from this point forward, we're done punishing ourselves. Okay?

BILL: Okay.

NANCY: Promise me.

BILL: I promise.

They embrace.

NANCY: This is the start of something good.

BILL: Do you think so?

NANCY: Yes. I can feel it.

(NANCY *holds* BILL. *Lights fade.*)

Scene 10

(*It is the next morning.* NANCY, *now wearing* BILL'*s grey sweatpants, enters from the kitchen. She starts to set the table. Light music is playing from her radio, also on the table.*)

NANCY: (*Calling out*) Honey! Breakfast is ready!

(NANCY *exits to the kitchen. A crash.*)

NANCY: (*Offstage*) Almost!

(*After a moment* BILL *enters, dressed in a suit and tie. The whole thing is oddly normal.* NANCY *enters and they look at one another.*)

BILL: Morning.

NANCY: Morning. Sleep well?

BILL: Like a log. You?

NANCY: The same.

BILL: I hope my snoring didn't bother you.

NANCY: What about your snoring?

BILL: It's chronic. I've tried everything to fix it but nothing seems to help.

NANCY: I didn't even notice it.

(BILL *goes to the table.*)

BILL: Do you have my paper?

NANCY: Right here.

(NANCY *brings* BILL *the paper.*)

BILL: Thank you.

BILL begins to read the paper.

NANCY: So. Do you have a busy day?

BILL: Yes.

NANCY: I bet you do. But then again I suppose every day at a hospital is.

BILL: I suppose so.

NANCY: *(Beat)* It's funny that you're a doctor.

BILL: Why is it funny?

NANCY: It's just ironic I guess. *(Beat)* What kind are you?

BILL: Why do you ask?

NANCY: Because I'm interested in who you are.

BILL: I'm a doctor, honey. That is all you need to know.

NANCY: *(Beat)* Can you at least tell me where you work?

BILL: Why?

NANCY: In case there's an emergency and I need to reach you.

BILL: There won't be. *(Beat)* So. What's on the agenda for today?

NANCY: Well, I don't really know. I suppose I could straighten things up around here.

BILL: If you'd like.

NANCY: And then I thought I'd cook us a big celebration dinner.

BILL: What are we celebrating?

NANCY: Us of course.

(NANCY *goes over and kisses* BILL.)

BILL: I'll eat a light lunch.

NANCY: You better. Where's the nearest grocery store?

BILL: Why?

NANCY: If I'm going to cook us a dinner I'll need to get food.

BILL: I'll pick stuff up on the way home from work.

NANCY: That's sweet of you but I don't mind doing the shopping. Oh, and if I'm gonna buy stuff I'll need some money.

BILL: Tell me what you'd like and I'll get it.

NANCY: Bill, I don't mind.

BILL: I know. But I insist.

(Pause)

NANCY: Well, Alright. For tonight I was thinking Pork.

BILL: I don't like Pork.

NANCY: Why, Bill? You Jewish?

BILL: I just don't like it.

NANCY: Then how about a brisket?

BILL: Brisket's great.

NANCY: Good. We can pair it with some green beans perhaps. Some asparagus too.

BILL: I prefer potatoes.

NANCY: Then potatoes it shall be. But really Bill I'm happy to—

BILL: Consider it done.

NANCY: What am I going to do about clothes?

BILL: I'll get you all the clothes you'll ever need.

NANCY: But you don't know my size.

BILL: You're an eight.

NANCY: I'll check on your breakfast. (*She exits. After a moment she returns with a pan. She puts the contents of the pan onto the plate in front of him.*) Here you go Bill. Hot out of the pan. I hope you like it.

BILL: What is it?

NANCY: Scrambled eggs. My mother's recipe. Her scrambled eggs were famous.

(BILL *looks at the plate.*)

BILL: Take them away.

NANCY: Is something wrong?

BILL: *I said take them away.*

(NANCY *quickly takes the plate away.*)

NANCY: Alright.

BILL: I'm sorry, Nancy. I should have told you.

NANCY: Told me what?

BILL: I don't like my eggs scrambled.

(*Pause*)

NANCY: It's fine. I can put something else on.

(BILL *gets up.*)

BILL: No. I've got to get going.

NANCY: When will you be home?

BILL: Five at the absolute latest.

NANCY: Okay.

BILL: You're not mad about the eggs, are you honey?

NANCY: Of course not. After all, they're just silly eggs.

BILL: Have I told you how beautiful you look today?

NANCY: You don't have to say that.

BILL: I do. Because I mean it.

NANCY: Thank you, Bill.

BILL: We're really doing this, aren't we?

(BILL *kisses* NANCY *and exits. She stands in the kitchen looking after him.*)

NANCY: Yes. I suppose we are.

(*Music from the radio rises. Lights slowly fade.*)

An Interlude

(*To show the passage of time*)

RADIO NEWS ANCHOR: (*V O*) And in local news, Police have a possible lead in the ongoing hunt for the butcher of Harbor Park, alleged to have killed eleven women in the central Texas area over the past two years. According to a police spokesperson articles of clothing and other personal affects were discovered late yesterday afternoon in a wooded area by a group a boy scouts and their troop leader who described the clothing as "showing a blatant disregard for the camping practice of leave no trace." A department official told members of the press that the items in question suggest the possibility of a new victim. Anyone who has information regarding any missing persons is urged to call police.

Scene 11

(*It is three weeks later. The upstairs is empty.*)

(*After a moment the front door opens and* BILL *enters, home from a long day at work.*)

BILL: Honey I'm home!

NANCY: *(Off)* Is that you Bill?! *(She enters wearing an apron and a new dress along with high heels, which she doesn't seem too comfortable wearing. She's very Suzie homemaker. She kisses him hello.)* Did you have a nice day?

BILL: Busy busy busy. You?

NANCY: Same as always. Dinner should be ready soon.

BILL: Wonderful. *(Beat)* May I have my evening Gin and tonic?

NANCY: Well you could. I mean I know how much you love your gin and tonics. But I was thinking maybe you could try something, new.

BILL: Something, new?

NANCY: How about a vodka martini?

BILL: *(Beat)* Sure.

NANCY: Great! It's ready and waiting in the fridge.

(NANCY exits to the kitchen to get the drink. BILL takes off his coat. Sits on the couch, looks around, exhales. After a few moments, she comes back with a martini glass.)

NANCY: Here you go, Bill.

(NANCY hands the glass to BILL.)

BILL: Thank you.

NANCY: Now I want you to know this is my first vodka martini so I hope it's okay.

BILL: I'm sure it's wonderful.

(BILL takes a sip. His face goes funny.)

NANCY: What?

BILL: How did you make it?

NANCY: I put a shot of vodka in a martini glass and the rest olive juice. Why? Is it not good?

BILL: No. It's fine. Just a little salty is all.

NANCY: I can make you another one if you'd like.

BILL: No. This is good. I needed more sodium in my diet anyway.

(BILL *takes another tiny sip of the martini.* NANCY *stands there looking at him.*)

BILL: Dinner ready soon?

NANCY: Uh-huh.

BILL: What are we having?

NANCY: Chicken.

BILL: Great. I like chicken.

(NANCY *stands looking at* BILL.)

BILL: Something on your mind?

NANCY: Not at all. Why?

BILL: Just seems like there is.

NANCY: There isn't. (*Beat*) It's just I spend all day getting things ready for you and I want make sure you're happy.

BILL: I am happy, Nancy.

NANCY: Good! Cause I want you to know these past three weeks have been the best of my life.

BILL: Mine too. In all honesty you've brought a whole new swirl of emotions out of me.

NANCY: Have I?

BILL: Yes. It's like a tidal wave of… normalness that's just enveloped me.

NANCY: Normal-ness?

BILL: I'm completely consumed by it. And you know what's even stranger?

NANCY: Than your normal-ness?

BILL: For the first time in decades I feel like a living breathing person and not some monster hiding behind a mask of—

NANCY: Normal-ness?

BILL: Plus I haven't had the desire to kill anyone for weeks. And it's all thanks to you.

NANCY: You make me feel really… normal too.

BILL: Great.

(NANCY *about to leave but she stops*)

NANCY: Since we're on the subject.

BILL: Yes?

NANCY: Well, I was thinking we could start to branch out.

BILL: Branch out how?

NANCY: Well, not that I haven't loved it, because I have, but every day for the past three weeks has been pretty similar.

BILL: How?

NANCY: I wake up, cook you breakfast, clean the house, sit on the couch, do the laundry, cook you dinner and wait for you to come home. And it's great. But just a little, routine.

BILL: I thought you liked routine?

NANCY: I do. But maybe one day this week we could try going out for dinner.

BILL: Going out for dinner? I wouldn't even know where to go.

NANCY: Well, I heard on the radio about this new Italian place downtown. They've got this new chef who came all the way from Italy.

BILL: Did he?

NANCY: He's supposed to really be something, Bill. If you'd be up for it I think it might be nice treat.

BILL: I don't care for restaurants.

NANCY: You don't?

BILL: Not at all. They're far too loud and expensive.

NANCY: Maybe we could get there early then. The ad said they've got this early bird special. It sounds very affordable.

BILL: Nancy.

NANCY: And if we did that it would be guaranteed to be quieter too.

BILL: Why go to a restaurant when your cooking is so much better?

NANCY: Thank you, Bill. But the point I'm trying to make is that—

BILL: Yes?

NANCY: The only thing I've done while living here is stay cooped up under this roof.

BILL: A lot of people don't have a roof over their head, Nancy. You should feel fortunate.

NANCY: I do. It's just I'd like to go outdoors every now and then.

BILL: You're free to come and go as you please. All I ask is that you don't talk to anyone or let anyone see you.

NANCY: That's just it, Bill! Since moving in the only person I've seen is you. The only person I've talked to is you.

BILL: Why talk to other people?

NANCY: Because people talking to people is what people do.

BILL: People don't know you like I do.

NANCY: I know they don't. But what I'm trying to say is—

BILL: What, Nancy? What are you trying to say?

NANCY: We just seem a tad cut off is all.

BILL: Cut off? Hardly. We have radio. Television. We get the newspaper delivered every day.

NANCY: But do we know the neighbors?

BILL: What's knowing the neighbors got to do with anything?

NANCY: It's normal to know your neighbors, Bill. Neighbors should know each other.

BILL: Why?

NANCY: Because that's the point of having neighbors.

BILL: I make it a point *not* to know my neighbors.

NANCY: But what if I want to know the neighbors?

BILL: Do you know what would happen if you met the neighbors?

NANCY: I don't know. We'd become friends.

BILL: And what do friends do, Nancy? They go over to each other's houses. They walk around each other's houses. And that's when they discover things!

NANCY: Bill, you're yelling.

BILL: You're damn right I'm yelling!!! Neighbors are trouble and we don't need trouble!!!

(*Pause*)

NANCY: I'll go check on the chicken.

BILL: Don't give me that.

NANCY: (*Reset*) What?

BILL: The attitude, Nancy. I'm trying to unwind from work and I don't need it.

NANCY: I'm not trying to impede your unwinding, Bill. I just don't understand why we can' talk about these things without violence erupting.

BILL: You made the decision to stay here. And if you don't like this lifestyle you are free to go.

NANCY: I didn't mean it like that Bill. It's just you don't talk to me about anything and it makes me feel like I don't count.

BILL: Listen. I know it's hard, but when the time is right I'll tell you everything.

NANCY: When?

BILL: Sooner than you realize. (*He* kisses *her.*) But until then we live like we have been, okay?

NANCY: Okay. But what do I do if someone comes to the door?

BILL: Don't answer it.

NANCY: But what if they come back?

BILL: Then don't answer it again.

NANCY: So I should just never answer the door?

BILL: Never answer the door. (*He gets up and walks to the kitchen.*)

NANCY: Where are you going?

BILL: I need another martini.

NANCY: I can get it.

BILL: No. That's alright.

(BILL *exits.* NANCY *stares at the front door.*)

Scene 12

(The next day. The upstairs is empty. The doorbell rings.
NANCY *enters, presumably from cleaning another room and*
stares at the door. It rings again. She walks a bit closer. Then
knocking. Through the door we hear JOANNE.)

JOANNE: *(Off)* Hello? Anybody home?

NANCY: Can I help you?

JOANNE: *(Off)* Hi! I'm your next door neighbor.

NANCY: Yes?

JOANNE: *(Off)* …I wanted to stop by and say welcome
to the neighborhood. Seeing as how you moved here a
month ago?

*(*NANCY *goes to the door.* JOANNE, *a woman in her mid-*
fifties holding a bunt cake.)

NANCY: Did you say we moved here a month ago?

JOANNE: I'm sorry, I would have come over sooner but
you how busy life can get. V F W balls, charity cook
outs, book clubs; next thing you know you look at the
calendar and it's four weeks later! *(Beat)* Anyway, I'll
just leave this with you. It's a bunt cake. I didn't know
if you had an egg allergy so I used substitute.

*(*JOANNE *hands* NANCY *the bunt cake.)*

JOANNE: *(Paired with an awkward wave)* Welcome to the
neighborhood. *(She turns to leave.)*

NANCY: Would you like to come in?

JOANNE: Oh. I don't want to intrude.

NANCY: No. You're not at all. Actually I was just
cleaning up.

JOANNE: Really I can come back another time.

NANCY: Now's fine. Please come in.

JOANNE: You sure?

NANCY: I insist.

JOANNE: Alright.

JOANNE enters the living room space.

JOANNE: I'm Joanne, by the way.

NANCY: I'm Nancy. *(Beat)* So we just moved in a month ago?

JOANNE: …Unless I'm mistaken?

NANCY: No. You're not. It's just my husband took care of all the details. He moved us in and had me come when it was ready.

JOANNE: Oh! I can understand that. Men just want to do everything, don't they?

NANCY: They certainly do.

JOANNE: Bless their hearts but sometimes they can be real control freaks. *(Beat)* I hope the move went well.

NANCY: It did. I hope it didn't disturb the neighborhood too much.

JOANNE: Not at all, dear! Matter of fact we hardly knew you were here at all. One day there's a for rent sign on the lawn, the next there's a car in the driveway and family moved in. I swear your husband must've moved in here during the dead of night!

NANCY: That's when he gets his best work done.

JOANNE: Mine too. Some night's my Roy doesn't even go to bed. Just stays up working. *(Taking in the space)* I've got to say, compared to the Hendersons, I just love the way you two have decorated this place.

NANCY: The Hendersons?

JOANNE: The folks who lived here before you. Lived here forty two years. And the way the place smelled you'd know it.

NANCY: That bad, huh?

JOANNE: Yep. After John passed things got away from Helda a little bit. Things stacked from floor to ceiling in every room. Awful dangerous way to live. I remember one time not seeing her a few days and fearing the worst I came over to see if anything had happened. Turned out the poor woman had locked herself in the basement storing preserves.

NANCY: You're kidding?

JOANNE: I wish I was. When the fire marshals opened the door there she was, madder than hell. She'd been down there screaming and shouting for about a day, but to no avail. Back in the Cuban Missile Crisis John had fortified the entire basement with lead and iron, making it bomb proof, missile proof and unfortunately for Helda, soundproof.

NANCY: It's a good thing you came over.

JOANNE: Helda didn't see it that way. She was very protective of her possessions and always thought someone was out to get her. I remember her telling me she knew exactly how many figurines were on her dresser and if one of them had so much as moved, she was gonna ring up the police. I told her not to bother, that if I wanted some mini porcelain horses all I'd have to do is call my aunt Betsy in Houston. (Beat) Anyway, seeing things so empty is a real breath of fresh air.

NANCY: I know it's a little bare, but we haven't quite moved in fully.

JOANNE: No. I didn't mean it like that! I just meant seeing a room this big so empty is—

NANCY: Unusual?

JOANNE: What I was going to say is your taste is very minimal.

NANCY: You think so?

JOANNE: Oh yes. It's very modern. *(Looking around realizing it's anything but)*. In a vintage kind of way.

NANCY: The vintage part is what my husband likes. I feel the place could use some brightening up.

JOANNE: Well if you need any help at all, I've been told I have a keen eye for interior decorating.

NANCY: Yeah?

JOANNE: Yes. Especially draping. Just last month I put up these magenta and blue drapes in my living room. Of course Roy thinks they're too bold, but talk about turning a space from a ehhh to a WOW!

NANCY: Can I offer you something to drink?

JOANNE: Oh that's very sweet of you but I can't stay for long. Got things to do and people to harass. *(Beat)* That was a joke.

NANCY: Oh. It was funny.

JOANNE: So where are you and your husband originally from?

NANCY: *(Forgetting)* What do you mean?

JOANNE: I mean where did you move from?

NANCY: Oh! Yes. We're from…Milwaukee.

JOANNE: Milwaukee?

NANCY: Yes.

JOANNE: That in Minnesota?

NANCY: Wisconsin.

JOANNE: That's funny. I could've sworn it was in Minnesota. But then again I've never been one for Geography. Or snow. Or the Midwest. *(Beat)* Either way this is a real treat!

NANCY: How so?

JOANNE: Well, I've never met anyone from Milwaukee, much less had them as neighbors. Tell me, what's it like?

NANCY: Milwaukee? I suppose it's kinda like down here.

JOANNE: Milwaukee is like Texas?

NANCY: Except here it's warmer and they're fewer trees.

JOANNE: Learn something new every day. So why'd you two move all the way here from all the way there?

NANCY: For my husband's work.

JOANNE: Oh. And what does he do?

NANCY: He's a doctor.

JOANNE: Oh! What kind?

NANCY: He's a… He's a…

JOANNE: I'm sorry. You don't have to answer that. I'm being completely rude. It's bad enough I come barging in here without warning but I ask you a million and one personal questions.

NANCY: I'm glad you came over. Truth is I could use the company. Since the move I've kinda been having a hard time.

JOANNE: I'm sorry to hear that. Why?

NANCY: I don't know. I mean for the longest time I dreamt of living here. Almost like this is where I always belonged. But now I just can't help feeling, isolated. It's almost as if I'm invisible. *(Beat)* Stupid, huh?

JOANNE: Absolutely not. I know exactly how you feel. It wasn't that long ago that I felt like an outsider too.

NANCY: What made it better?

JOANNE: I needed to feel like I belonged. *(Beat)* And I know just the thing. *(She heads for the front door.)*

NANCY: Where are you going?

JOANNE: Be back in a jif! Mean time get a glass of water! *(She exits.)*

NANCY: A glass of water?

JOANNE: *(Off stage)* A big one!

(NANCY gets a big glass of water.)

(JOANNE returns with some with a freshly cut flowers. She walks to NANCY and plops some of them into the glass.)

JOANNE: Ta-Da!

NANCY: Roses?

JOANNE: Fresh cut from my garden!

NANCY: Oh Joanne I don't want to take your flowers.

JOANNE: It's fine. I always cut more than I need and these were sitting out in my basket waiting for a home. Do you like them?

NANCY: I love them! *(Beat)* Where should we put them?

JOANNE: How about here on the table. *(She put flowers on the table.)* There! It's official. You belong.

NANCY: Thank you for the flowers, Joanne. I can't tell you how much I appreciate it. *(Seems to hit home for her. She's almost crying.)*

JOANNE: Say. Is everything alright?

NANCY: Of course. These are tears of joy.

JOANNE: Okay. Just for a moment you seemed a little—

NANCY: What?

JOANNE: Sad.

NANCY: No. Not at all. I'm very happy. It's just Bill and I, that's my husband, we haven't been married long and with the move and all it's a little overwhelming.

JOANNE: Marriage isn't always easy, believe you me. But in the end it's worth it. That is, if you can exist without murdering each other. So far Roy and I are still here.

NANCY: How long have you and Roy been married?

JOANNE: A long time. Longer than I care to admit.

NANCY: And are you two happy?

JOANNE: Even when we're not. *(Beat)* You and your Bill, you're happy, aren't ya?

NANCY: Of course. It's just, sometimes I feel like I'm not being heard. And it's frustrating.

JOANNE: I'm going to give you advice someone should have given me when I was your age. *(Beat)* When you're feeling frustrated, sometimes the best thing to do is take control.

NANCY: You make it sound so easy.

JOANNE: That's because it is. Trust me. When Roy and I were first married, he had this thing about mowing the lawn, which in itself isn't bad, except that he had a nasty habit of mowing right over my prize winning tulips. It's not that he was doing it intentionally, just he's always been a tad nearsighted. No matter how much I begged him to stop mowing, he wouldn't. Said a man needs to take care of his lawn and if a few tulips get slayed in the process then so be it. So one day I got a bucket full of rocks and spread them all around the lawn. I'll never forget Roy coming into the house, face red as a beet, yelling about the mower being wrecked due to rocks all over the lawn. I told him a woman needs to take care of her tulips and if a lawn mower gets wrecked in the process, then so be it. *(Beat)*

After that not only were my tulips safe, but Roy never touched that mower again. Moral of the story, when something's bothering you, it's best to show rather than tell. *(Beat)* Well, I hate to cut and run but I've got a turkey in the oven that needs basting. Lord knows Roy would throw a fit if his poultry wasn't moist. *(Beat)* You're sure you're okay?

NANCY: Absolutely.

JOANNE: That's what I like to hear. See ya later, neighbor! And enjoy the bunt cake.

NANCY: We will.

(JOANNE goes to the door.)

NANCY: Say Joanne?

JOANNE: Yes?

NANCY: Would you and Roy like to come over for dinner some time?

JOANNE: Like to? We'd love to!

NANCY: Great. How about tomorrow?

JOANNE: Let's see. Tonight is Garden club. Wednesday's Key Club, Thursday's the wheelchair banquet, Friday's the A S P C A fund raiser… Tomorrow we're free.

NANCY: How's six sound?

JOANNE: Perfect!

NANCY: Great.

JOANNE: You and me Nancy. We're gonna be great friends. I can feel it!

(JOANNE exits. NANCY goes to the flowers and picks them up. She looks at them and smiles.)

NANCY: I hope so.

(Lights fade.)

Scene 13

(Morning in the breakfast nook. BILL *is sitting at the table reading the newspaper.* NANCY *enters from preparing breakfast in the kitchen. There is music playing on the radio.)*

NANCY: Bill?

BILL: *(Still reading the paper)* Hmm?

(After a moment, NANCY *goes to the radio and turns it off. She then turns to* BILL, *who is unaffected by the change.)*

NANCY: Bill.

BILL: I heard you the first time.

NANCY: I'd like you to look at me.

*(*BILL *puts down the paper and looks to* NANCY. *She is busy setting places on the table for him and herself.)*

BILL: What is it?

NANCY: We're happy, right?

BILL: Of course. Why?

NANCY: I'm just asking.

BILL: Are you mad about other evening?

NANCY: Nope.

BILL: You're sure. Because if there's anything I can do—

NANCY: Nope.

BILL: Good.

*(*BILL *goes back to reading the paper.* NANCY *is finished setting places.)*

NANCY: But I am wondering something.

BILL: Yes?

NANCY: Do you think we'll ever get married?

BILL: What?

NANCY: I don't mean right now, per se. But some time in the future.

BILL: That's hard to say. We've barely known each other three weeks.

NANCY: Do you trust me?

BILL: Yes.

NANCY: I mean do you trust that I'd never do anything to hurt you.

BILL: Of course.

NANCY: So if I told you I knew some things, you wouldn't get mad, would you?

(BILL *puts down the paper.*)

BILL: What sort of things?

NANCY: Well, for example. I know that you moved here a month ago.

BILL: And how do you know that?

NANCY: Because our neighbor stopped by. (*She exits to kitchen.*)

BILL: What?

(NANCY *returns with roses. She places them on living room table and sits on couch.*)

NANCY: She wanted to welcome us to the neighborhood.

BILL: You opened the door?

NANCY: Yes.

BILL: I told you not to open the door.

NANCY: I know you did. But I did it anyway.

BILL: You didn't let her in here, did you?

NANCY: Well I thought it would be rude not to.

BILL: Nancy! What did I tell you?

NANCY: It was fine, Bill. She's perfectly harmless.

BILL: I don't care. You shouldn't have opened the door.

NANCY: And you should have told me we moved here a month ago.

BILL: We didn't move here a month ago. I did.

NANCY: And then you kidnapped me.

BILL: Yes.

NANCY: Did you know the basement used to be a bomb shelter?

BILL: What?

NANCY: Joanne, that's our neighbor, she told me the people who lived in this house turned the basement into a bomb shelter. Is that why you moved here?

BILL: I don't want to talk about it.

(Pause)

NANCY: Is moving around part of your strategy of not getting caught?

BILL: I'm not talking about that either.

NANCY: Why not?

BILL: Because it's in the past. Now pour the coffee.

(NANCY brings the coffee pot to the table.)

NANCY: Did you move every time you killed a woman?

BILL: Nancy…

NANCY: Do you change your name? Do you change your job? Do you even have a driver's license?

BILL: Aren't we supposed to be starting over?

NANCY: Of course we are.

BILL: Then pour the coffee. Please.

NANCY: Alright, Bill. Fine. If you don't want to talk I can't force you to. But there are going to be some changes.

BILL: What sort of changes?

NANCY: Well. You might enjoy living this way. Hiding from the world. Hiding from me. But I'm done hiding.

BILL: What are you going to do?

NANCY: It's not what I'm going to do. It's what we're going to do.

BILL: And what are we going to do?

NANCY: Tonight we're having the neighbors over for dinner. Tell me when to stop.

(NANCY *begins to pour coffee for* BILL.)

BILL: Do you see what happens?

NANCY: Bill—

BILL: Do you see how things progress?

NANCY: It's getting full, Bill.

BILL: Then stop pouring!

(NANCY *stops.*)

NANCY: There's still room for cream.

BILL: I told you not to open the door Nancy. I told you not to talk to anyone. But did you listen?

NANCY: Normal people have their neighbors over for dinner, Bill.

BILL: We're not having the neighbors over for dinner—

NANCY: —I really think you /should—

BILL: —and that's/ *final.*

(BILL *returns to his paper.* NANCY *exits and returns to cooking breakfast. After a moment)*

BILL: Are you mad at me?

NANCY *(Off. Cheerful)* What?

BILL: Are you mad at me?

(NANCY enters with the cooking pan which she brings over to BILL.)

NANCY: Of course not, baby cakes. You're my little honey muffin and I love you. Now eat your breakfast before it gets cold.

(NANCY flops the contents onto BILL's plate and returns to the stove to clean up. He looks at the plate.)

BILL: What's this?

NANCY: It's your breakfast, of course. Scrambled eggs.

BILL: I told you I don't like scrambled eggs.

NANCY: Sorry. I must've forgot.

BILL: Take them away.

NANCY: Why?

BILL: Because I'm not eating them.

NANCY: Yes you are.

(NANCY picks up BILL's fork.)

BILL: Nancy—

(NANCY stabs the fork through BILL's hand and sticks it into the table. He doesn't react other than looking at the fork.)

NANCY: I put a lot of effort into making those eggs and not only are you going to eat them but you're going to enjoy them. Oh, and if you could come home a little bit earlier I'd appreciate it. We want to be more than ready for our dinner with the neighbors.

BILL: What are we having?

NANCY: Pot roast. Originally I was thinking salmon, but I know how finicky you get around seafood.

BILL: What time should I be home?

NANCY: I told them to come at six, so five should do it.
(Beat) By the way— We're married and we just moved
here from Wisconsin. That's what I told Joanne when
she asked when she asked where we're from.

BILL: I'm from Cleveland.

NANCY: Well guess what sweetie pie? Now you're
from Milwaukee. And in the future it might be good to
be on the same page about these sorts of things.

(Pause)

BILL: About tonight—

NANCY: You're going to behave. We're gonna be the
perfect couple and if we're not there's going to be hell
to pay. Do you understand?

BILL: Do you want to get the groceries or should I?

NANCY: I already did. Here's your credit card.

*(NANCY puts the card on the table. BILL takes the fork out of
his hand and takes a bite of his eggs. Lights fade.)*

Scene 14

*(It is the next evening. We are in the living room. BILL
enters through the front door. He is wearing a suit and tie
and also has a big bandage wrapped around the hand that
was stabbed. He takes off his coat and hangs it by the door.
The house is strangely quiet, which he notices.)*

BILL: Nancy?

*(After a moment NANCY enters from the kitchen. She's
dressed for a dinner party, which may or may not be too
dressed up. She's also wearing an apron and holding a
martini.)*

BILL: You look nice.

NANCY: I told you to be home at five.

BILL: And?

NANCY: You're late.

BILL: Am I?

NANCY: By twenty six minutes.

BILL: Sorry. I was held up at work.

NANCY: It's fine, darling. But in the future, call. *(Beat)* I made you a drink.

BILL: What is it?

NANCY: A martini.

(BILL *walks up to* NANCY *and takes the glass.*)

BILL: Thank you.

NANCY: Drink up.

(BILL *looks at* NANCY *and hesitantly takes a sip. After realizing it's not terrible he takes a bigger sip, eventually drinking the whole thing.*)

NANCY: Good?

BILL: A little stiff. But yes.

NANCY: Good. Make yourself comfortable.

BILL: Nancy?

NANCY: Hmm?

BILL: What's going on?

NANCY: What's going on is I'm going to check the meat. I'd be so embarrassed if it got overcooked—

BILL: I meant with how you're acting.

NANCY: How am I acting?

BILL: Strange.

NANCY: I suppose I am. But then again so are you so I guess we're even aren't we?

BILL: I don't like this.

NANCY: I'm sorry to hear that but we really don't have time to discuss it. We've got a dinner party to get ready for.

BILL: I want you to cancel.

NANCY: But they're due any minute.

BILL: I don't care. I want you to call this thing off, Nancy. I want to—

(Doorbell rings.)

NANCY: Looks like they're early.

BILL: Whatever this is, Nancy. We need to talk about it before things go too far.

NANCY: Get the door.

(NANCY takes the martini glass and heads into the kitchen. BILL prepares himself, goes to the door and opens it to JOANNE, who is dressed up and wearing makeup. She is wearing a wrap.)

BILL: *(Completely normal and inviting)* Hi. You must be Joanne.

JOANNE: That's me. And you must be…

BILL: I'm Nancy's husband. Bill.

JOANNE: Nice to meet you!

BILL: *(Pause)* Please come in.

(JOANNE enters and BILL closes the door.)

JOANNE: Sorry for standing there like a dolt. I just need to be invited in. It's just my German upbringing.

BILL: Ah. *Sie sind aus Deutschland?*

JOANNE: …

BILL: I asked if you were German.

JOANNE: Oh! Lord No! No, but my parents were. What about you? Are you German?

BILL: Me? No…I just speak the language.

JOANNE: Well, how about that? Not only are you a doctor but you speak a foreign language. Nancy really hit the lottery, didn't she?

BILL: She certainly did.

JOANNE: I'll tell you though, the language to learn is Spanish. They say in ten years half the population won't even know how to speak English.

BILL: That's why I also speak Spanish.

JOANNE: Do you really?

BILL: *Si. (Beat)* Can I take your wrap?

JOANNE: *Gracias.*

(JOANNE hands BILL her wrap. She notices the bandage on his hand.)

JOANNE: My! What happened to your hand?

BILL: Nothing. Just a little mishap at work.

JOANNE: It looks like more than a mishap. But I suppose you'd know about it more than I, you being a doctor and all.

BILL: So I was told we'd be entertaining you and your husband?

JOANNE: That was the plan. But in my household plans change like the wind.

BILL: You're husband couldn't make it?

JOANNE: Sadly not. But Roy really wanted to. Unfortunately he got called into work.

BILL: Sounds like your husband is a dedicated man.

JOANNE: He certainly is. Now if only he were dedicated to me… Joking!

BILL: Oh that was funny.

JOANNE: Sorry. I can be a tad brash. People say I got a sense of humor like a bull whip.

(NANCY *enters.*)

NANCY: I thought I heard the doorbell. Hi Joanne. How are you?

JOANNE: Oh you know me. Chugging along.

NANCY: Look at how nice you're dressed.

JOANNE: Me? Look at you. If I'd known this was such a fancy occasion I'd of put on makeup.

NANCY: Please, you look wonderful. The reason I'm so dressed up is this is the first time we've had company.

JOANNE: Since you've been in town, you mean?

NANCY: Since we've been married.

JOANNE: You're kidding?

NANCY: No, sadly we just haven't had time for friends. But we're trying to change that, aren't we honey?

JOANNE: And how long have you two been married for?

NANCY: How long has it been, sweetie? A year? A year and a half?

BILL: Three weeks.

(*Awkward pause.* NANCY *breaks the tension with laughter.*)

NANCY: Oh, Bill. Such a kidder. His sense of humor is the biggest reason why I fell in love with him. (*Beat*) So where's Roy?

BILL: I'm afraid Roy couldn't make it, dear.

NANCY: Oh no! Really?

JOANNE: Yep, sadly so. Got called off to work.

NANCY: Well, that's alright. We'll just have to do this again, won't we dear?

JOANNE: So tell me, how did you two meet?

NANCY: It's long story.

JOANNE: If you don't mind telling it I'd love to hear it.

NANCY: Why don't you tell her, honey?

BILL: I'd prefer if you did.

NANCY: But you tell the story so much better.

BILL: I'm not in the mood.

NANCY: Oh come on, sweetie. We're entertaining. And this is what people who entertain do. They tell stories.

BILL: Not that story.

JOANNE: If it's a sensitive subject we don't have to discuss it.

NANCY: It's not at all. If Bill doesn't want to tell you I will. We met because he kidnapped me in a park and dragged me into his basement. I guess you could say the rest is history.

(This is very odd and JOANNE *has no idea what to make of it.)*

BILL: She's kidding. We met while I was in med school. In Milwaukee.

(Completely relieved JOANNE *begins to laugh.* BILL *and* NANCY *don't.)*

JOANNE: My! You had me going for a moment.

BILL: We like to kid around a lot.

NANCY: It brings joy to our otherwise dull existence. That's what Bill's dad used to say. He was a joke-ster too. And then he drowned in a sail boating accident…

JOANNE: Did you say drowned?

NANCY: Yes. Sadly I did. The man was a champion sailor but couldn't swim to save his life. The whole thing could have been avoided if he'd been wearing

a life vest. But then again, he did get hit by a rogue
wave. Well, the meat should be done any second now.
Anyone care for a pre-dinner drink?

BILL: I'll take another martini.

NANCY: Joanne?

JOANNE: A glass of wine if you have it.

NANCY: Red or white?

JOANNE: White.

NANCY: Coming right up.

JOANNE: Where's your rest room? I'd like to freshen up
before dinner.

NANCY: Of course. Down the hall. First door on the
right.

JOANNE: I'll be right back.

NANCY: Don't keep us waiting too long.

(JOANNE *exits.*)

NANCY: Nice, isn't she?

BILL: What was that comment about my father?

NANCY: It's called detail honey. It's necessary when
trying to sell an illusion.

BILL: I don't like how you're acting.

NANCY: I'm sorry, Bill. I guess I'm just trying to get
used to my new role as the typical housewife.

BILL: I never said I wanted that.

NANCY: That's funny. Because that's how you treat me.

BILL: How do I treat you?

NANCY: This isn't the time to discuss it. We're
entertaining.

BILL: Not any longer. When she comes back tell her
you're not feeling well.

NANCY: When she comes back from the bathroom we are going to sit down and we are going to tell her all about us.

BILL: What do you mean "all about us"?

NANCY: I'm going to tell her about our wedding, about your family, about my family, how our uncles once got in a fist fight over the last hot dog at the fourth of July barbecue but now they're the best of pals.

BILL: So you just want you make everything up?

NANCY: I want things to be real, Bill. But they're not and it's killing me.

BILL: I need more time.

NANCY: Ever since I came upstairs that's all you've said, all while putting on this facade of being a normal doctor.

BILL: I am a normal doctor.

NANCY: You're a serial killer!!!

BILL: Keep your voice down. She'll hear you.

NANCY: Then let her hear me. Let the whole fucking world hear me! I don't care anymore.

BILL: What do you want?!

NANCY: I want the real you. The man who abducted me in the park. The man who tied me up in the basement. The man who stabbed me in the leg and tended to my wounds.

BILL: I want to give you a future, Nancy. But I can't be a serial killer and do that.

NANCY: Then I don't want a future!

BILL: (*Beat*) Look. We're going to figure this out. But whatever this is, it's not solving anything. Now get rid of her.

NANCY: But honey bunny? We don't want to be rude. I mean we haven't even eaten yet.

BILL: I'm being serious, Nancy.

NANCY: How about we have a drink and go from there.

(BILL *grabs her by the arm.*)

BILL: Get. Her. Out. Of. Here.

NANCY: What are you going to do if I don't?

BILL: You don't want to find out.

NANCY: You gonna kill her? Chop her up and throw her in the river like you did everyone else?

BILL: You'd like that wouldn't you?

NANCY: Maybe I would.

(JOANNE *enters.*)

JOANNE: Hello.

(BILL *lets go of* NANCY's *arm.*)

NANCY: I'll go get those drinks.

(NANCY *exits.* BILL *and* JOANNE *sit in silence for a few moments.*)

BILL: I'm sorry about that. We were just—

JOANNE: No explanation needed. Lovers' quarrels are part of any healthy marriage. In the beginning, Roy and I used to fight like cats and dogs all the time. At the time it was tough, but in retrospect is wasn't so bad. The bigger the fight the better the making up. *(Beat)* So how are you adjusting to the lone star state?

BILL: Texas has an undeniable charm.

JOANNE: It certainly does. *(Beat)* Ten years ago Roy and I moved to California for his work. Los Angeles to be exact. At first it was nice with the palm trees and all but we found ourselves missing the warmth and kindness that only Texans can offer, so here we are. Plus Roy really missed his Texas barbecue.

BILL: And what does your husband do?

JOANNE: Oh, he's a cop.

(NANCY *enters with a martini and a glass of white wine.*)

NANCY: It's going to be a few more minutes on the roast. Everybody getting along?

BILL: Quite well.

(*Handing* BILL *his martini:*)

NANCY: Good.

BILL: Matter of fact the conversation just took a very interesting turn.

NANCY: Did it?

JOANNE: Not really. We were just talking about my husband's job.

NANCY: And what's that?

BILL: He's a cop.

(*Pause*)

NANCY: A cop. I feel safer already. What kind of cop is Roy?

(NANCY *hands* JOANNE *her wine glass.*)

JOANNE: Well, he's not really a cop anymore.

NANCY: He's retired?

JOANNE: Oh no. He's active duty. Just not like in California. Back then he was on the beat. Patrolled some pretty bad neighborhoods, too. Which made me a wreck. Every morning I'd hand him his lunch, kiss him goodbye and watch him walk out that front door, wondering if he was going to come back. (*beat*) Well, those days are far behind us now. Now he's more of a specialist.

NANCY: What does he specialize in?

JOANNE: Serial killers.

NANCY: Serial killers? That sounds pretty serious, huh, Bill?

JOANNE: It certainly is. Roy's suited for it too. He's always been a thinker, and catching a serial killer requires a great deal of thought.

NANCY: Too bad there aren't any serial killers around these parts to keep your husband busy.

BILL: Honey do you want to check the meat?

NANCY: The meat has five more minutes. Besides I want to hear more about serial killers.

BILL: It's not appropriate discussion.

JOANNE: Oh please. I don't mind at all! I've been prying into your lives so the least I can do is tell you about mine.

NANCY: You're not a serial killer, are you Joanne?

(NANCY and JOANNE have a momentary laugh. BILL is dead calm.)

JOANNE: Oh no. Not me. But there is one in the city.

NANCY: Is there?

JOANNE: The past two years he's kidnapped eleven women. Killed em all, chopped em up and dumped their remains in the river with a poem.

NANCY: With a poem?

JOANNE: Yes. Herald's published the last few.

NANCY: Wait a minute. I think I saw that. If I remember correctly they were pretty good.

JOANNE: They weren't half bad. I'll give him that much.

NANCY: Why do you think he does it?

JOANNE: Killing all those women?

NANCY: Writing the poems.

JOANNE: I don't really know. I mean clearly he wants people to read em otherwise he wouldn't write em. Probably looking for his fifteen minutes of fame.

BILL: Or perhaps he's writing them for his victims.

JOANNE: Writing them for the victims?

BILL: Maybe it's his way of honoring them.

JOANNE: Honoring his victims...I suppose it could be that. Personally I always figured it was more simple. Most of these serial killers like to leave something behind to let the police know who did it. More times than not it even offers a clue as to who they are. Years ago there was one killer who used to leave behind bars of soap. When he got caught the cops asked him why he did that. Turned out the fella worked at a soap factory. *(Beat)* Can you imagine?

BILL: Maybe our killer works at a poetry factory.

JOANNE: A poetry factory!

(NANCY and JOANNE laugh. BILL stays quiet.)

JOANNE: Well...we'll find out why he leaves the poems behind soon enough.

(BILL looks at JOANNE very seriously.)

NANCY: How's that?

JOANNE: I've been sworn to secrecy. But I might as well tell you two. They just got him.

(Pause)

BILL: I'm sorry?

JOANNE: Actually that's why Roy couldn't make it tonight. Not more than two hours ago the fella walked right into the police station and confessed to the whole thing.

(Pause)

NANCY: Why would anyone confess to such a horrible crime spree?

JOANNE: So he can take credit for his work. *(Beat)* According to Roy, for the past two years this nut has been doing his life's work. By turning himself in he's taking credit for it.

NANCY: I still don't see why he'd want to—

JOANNE: The same as with the poems. So he can be recognized. No matter how sad or happy, how crazy or deranged, we all want to be seen and heard.

NANCY: I guess we do, don't we?

JOANNE: Of course we do. It's human nature. Just most of us tend not to hack each other up to do so. I'll tell you. The world today is a scary place.

(A strange silence. NANCY gets up.)

NANCY: This calls for a celebration.

BILL: What does?

NANCY: Now that the crazy manic is caught we can move on with our lives.

JOANNE: Yes. I suppose you're right.

NANCY: I think I smell that pot roast. Give me a few minutes and dinner will be served.

(NANCY gets up and goes to the kitchen. JOANNE and BILL sit in silence. He is staring at her.)

JOANNE: Well, I sure am hungry. *(Silence)* I can't tell you how nice it is to meet you and your wife. It's a relief to get some fresh blood into the neighborhood.

BILL: We're not married.

JOANNE: Pardon?

BILL: It's easy to go around guessing why people do what they do, but when it comes down to it, you don't know a thing about it.

JOANNE: Bill, if I've said something to offend you I'm sorry.

BILL: Joanne, you couldn't offend me if you tried.

JOANNE: *(Beat)* Well, good.

BILL: But I do have one question.

JOANNE: Sure.

BILL: How does Roy know they got him?

JOANNE: Got who?

BILL: The maniac killer.

JOANNE: Well… Because like I said, he walked right into the police station. *(A strange pause)* Maybe we should switch to a lighter topic…

BILL: Let me clarify something. This man has sacrificed two years of his life showing the world just how filthy and dirty and false it truly is. And now he's going to just walk into a police station and turn himself in?

JOANNE: I don't see why he wouldn't.

BILL: Because his work isn't finished.

(Beat)

JOANNE: Bill. You're not making any—

BILL: There are supposed to be twelve. And there will be. *(Beat)* I suggest you leave before I lose my composure.

(JOANNE gets up.)

JOANNE: I'm suddenly not feeling very well. I think I'll be leaving. *(She gets the fuck out of the house. She doesn't even close the door.)*

(Very calmly, BILL goes to the front door and shuts it. He then looks around a moment, and undresses. He then opens the door to the basement and walks down the staircase.)

(A moment of silence. NANCY enters.)

NANCY: Alright the candles are lit and dinner is on the...table.

(NANCY notices BILL's clothes on the table. She goes over to them.)

NANCY: Bill? *(Beat)* Bill??

(We hear footsteps coming up the staircase. NANCY stands silent and waits. The door to the basement opens and BILL, backlit by an orange grow, appears at the top of the basement staircase.)

NANCY: Where's Joanne?

BILL: She left.

NANCY: You told her, didn't you?

BILL: I can't have people taking credit for my work. Especially when it isn't done.

NANCY: I thought your work was finished.

BILL: Soon.

(Slight pause)

NANCY: I don't suppose it would've worked anyway. Thinking about it I don't know I even wanted it to. All this time I've been searching for this thing.

BILL: And what is that, Nancy?

NANCY: I wanted to know that there's something more.

BILL: Maybe there is. *(Beat. He kisses her.)* Are you scared?

NANCY: I don't know that I am. Do you want me to be?

(BILL and NANCY go into the basement, closing the door behind them.)

(Lights slowly fade.)

END OF PLAY

www.ingramcontent.com/pod-product-compliance
Lightning Source LLC
Chambersburg PA
CBHW052215090426
42741CB00010B/2545